# The
# TAROT
## *Journal*

### Your Personal Voyage of Self-Discovery

summersdale

THE TAROT JOURNAL

Text by El Clarke

An Hachette UK Company
www.hachette.co.uk

Summersdale Publishers Ltd
Part of Octopus Publishing Group Limited
Carmelite House
50 Victoria Embankment
LONDON
EC4Y 0DZ
UK

www.summersdale.com

Printed and bound in China

ISBN: 978-1-80007-678-5

Substantial discounts on bulk quantities of Summersdale books are available to corporations, professional associations and other organizations. For details contact general enquiries: telephone: +44 (0) 1243 771107 or email: enquiries@summersdale.com.

Name:

..........................................................................................

Date of birth:

..........................................................................................

Star sign:

..........................................................................................

Favourite card:

..........................................................................................

Date journal started:

..........................................................................................

Goal:

..........................................................................................

..........................................................................................

..........................................................................................

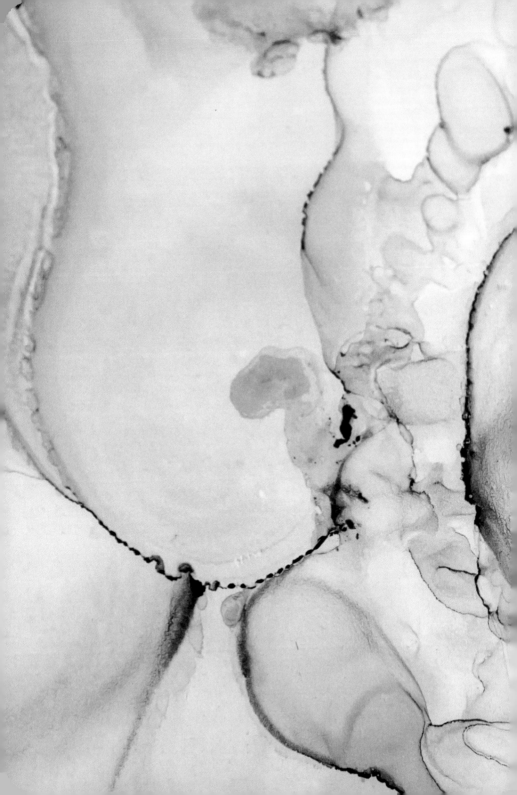

# INTRODUCTION

Welcome to your guided tarot journal.

Once you discover the joy and power of working with the tarot, you'll find the cards invaluable in guiding you through life's ups and downs. From enhancing your self-care practices to revealing what the future may hold, they are a powerful tool for reflection as well as divination.

This beautiful little book gives you an overview of what the tarot are for, and introduces some of the many ways in which these cards can be used. The different cards and their meanings are all explained, providing you with a quick way to reference the interpretation of your reading. The journal is divided into sections such as Reflection, Divination, Self-Care and Friendship, with an example spread suggested for each theme. There is space for you to fill in which cards come up, so you can keep a record of your tarot practice and maybe start to notice some familiar friends who keep cropping up for you. Finally, once you have developed your skills, there is a more free-form journal section at the back of the book with prompts for your practice and additional space to record your daily readings. So grab your tarot cards, and let's start our journey...

# A BRIEF HISTORY OF TAROT

Tarot cards were created by artists in Italy during the fourteenth century. They began with the addition of a new suit to the traditional deck of 52 playing cards. This suit was originally known as trump or triumph cards, commissioned by wealthy members of society to represent their family members and friends. Before the advent of the printing press only a privileged few could have owned the highly illustrated cards, which were painted by hand.

Early in their history, these cards were used exclusively as a parlour game. The use of cards for divination (fortune telling) is thought to have developed in the sixteenth and seventeenth centuries. The first tarot deck designed specifically for divinatory purposes was released in 1791. Tarot are just one among many tools used for divination, such as the reading of tea leaves. Over time, though, their use has expanded to answer questions about the past and present too. For many, tarot cards are the most trusted divination tool.

Tarot decks are divided into two groups, known as the major arcana and the minor arcana. The minor arcana is divided up into four suits, with 52 cards in total, much like a traditional deck of playing cards. These suits are Wands (sometimes called staves), Cups, Swords and Pentacles (also known as coins). Each of the suits is associated with a different area of your life, and the individual cards' meanings reflect this. The major arcana is made up of 22 different cards, each with their own unique design and meaning.

Unlike playing cards, which may have a decorative back but which tend to have a fairly consistent design, the artwork of a tarot deck has a great deal of importance too. Many artists and illustrators have created beautiful tarot decks, with their own interpretations of the different suits and the cards of the major arcana. The range is phenomenal, so when you are looking for a deck for yourself you are bound to find one whose artwork speaks to you.

When a reading shows mostly minor arcana cards, then your fate is considered to be in your own hands. If there are more major arcana cards revealed, destiny has more of a hand in your answer.

The cards are read in different spreads, ranging from a very simple three cards – representing the past, present and future – to complicated multi-card spreads, like the fan spread, which give you more detailed insight into your question or focus. As well as using spreads, you can take a single card for the day to reflect on your current situation.

They have traditionally been used by one person reading for another, but reading your own cards has become increasingly popular and can be a great way to hone your practice. It is also common for people to use tarot reading as part of their self-care, helping provide a focus to daily routine.

However you choose to use your tarot, this journal will give you guidance and space to develop your practice in a way that feels right for you.

# THE CARDS

## The Minor Arcana

With 52 cards in the minor arcana and 22 in the major, the tarot can seem like a difficult thing to learn, but much of reading the cards is intuitive. In this section, we will discuss the cards in a little more detail, including outlining the links that some cards have with various zodiac signs and planets as well as the four elements.

The suit of Wands is comparable to clubs in a deck of playing cards. It is associated with the element of fire, often showing the influence of the zodiac signs Aries, Leo and Sagittarius. These cards are about enterprise, work, creativity and growth.

The suit of Cups would be the hearts in a standard deck of cards. This suit is ruled by water and related to the zodiac signs Cancer, Scorpio and Pisces. The Cups are associated with the emotions, and if your reading mainly has Cups revealed, the issue at hand is likely to be one of the heart.

The suit of Swords is the equivalent to the spades in a deck of playing cards, linked by the Italian word for sword, *spada*. It is connected to the element of air, and shows the influence of Gemini, Libra and Aquarius. The Swords are concerned with mental activity, difficulties and troubles.

The Pentacles are the equivalent of diamonds in a set of playing cards. The suit is related to the element of earth and corresponds to the zodiac signs Taurus, Virgo and Capricorn. This suit is associated with money, land and prosperity.

## The Major Arcana

The major arcana is different to the minor, and less familiar as it does not have any links to a standard set of playing cards. There are 22 major arcana cards, each with its own symbolic image and meaning. These meanings are not always obvious, for example the Death card can signify transformation or change, which can be very positive.

All of the cards also have double meanings, depending on whether they are drawn upright or reversed. This adds another element of interpretation to every reading.

# THE MAJOR ARCANA

## 0 The Fool

This card is much like the joker in a deck of playing cards. Unnumbered, the Fool represents the spirit of chaos and the unknown. The card also represents innocence and the simple joy of living. It is governed by air and Uranus, further reiterating the Fool as a free spirit and bringer of the unexpected.

**Meaning:** You are safe to do whatever you need to, now is the time to take a risk. This may be the start of a new chapter for you. Unconventional people may be about to enter your life. This could be a sign of a need to explore or a desire for adventure. Expect the unexpected.

**Reversed meaning:** Foolishness or rash behaviour – look before you leap. Could also point to an irresponsible person.

## I The Magician

Representing a travelling entertainer of the sort that was common in medieval Europe, the Magician is at the centre of things. The card is associated with creativity, positive action and individuality. It is ruled by Mercury.

**Meaning:** New beginnings, perhaps the start of a new cycle in your life. A sense of purpose, determination and initiative. Most of all, potential, a sign to pay attention to your inner power.

**Reversed meaning:** Caution against pride and overinflated ego. Deception and tricks – a warning to be careful who you trust.

## II The High Priestess

This robed woman can have links to the Virgin Mary, the goddess Isis or the Moon goddess. She stands between pillars which represent duality. She is associated with the balance between life and death, and with virginity.

**Meaning:** A secret is soon to be revealed. This card has a strong feminine influence. It shows psychic ability and mystic power, and is associated with the unconscious mind, memory and intuition. It tells you to rely on your intuition rather than logic.

**Reversed meaning:** Use discretion. There are hidden obstacles at play and you may need to put off your plans. A lack of self-belief or painful secrets.

## III The Empress

The number three is of particular significance, symbolizing harmony, childbirth and maternal nature. Can be linked to the goddess Venus, and is usually shown wearing a crown with twelve stars, one for each sign of the zodiac. It is associated with the spring.

**Meaning:** May be related to childbirth and motherhood, but also to abundance and comfort. A sense of protection and security, nurturing, reassurance and a good foundation for the future. Also refers to fertility in the sense of creative ideas.

**Reversed meaning:** May signify issues with pregnancy, but more often being over-protective or overbearing. Can point to emotional blackmail. A need to spend more time in nature, or engage in activities that boost your creative energy.

## IV The Emperor

The Emperor represents a regal male figure, and is linked to power and aspiration. The card is ruled by Aries, so rams often appear in the Emperor's artwork. Can signify an important man, perhaps a father.

**Meaning:** Reaching your goals and the achievement of an ambition. May relate to authority or an influential masculine figure whose help is needed.

**Reversed meaning:** Unfulfilled ambitions, a craving for greater status. Overbearing behaviour and the abuse of power. Maybe you are being held back by someone who is weak-willed or unambitious, or this could be a part of yourself.

## V The Hierophant

This card is the masculine companion to the High Priestess. Connected to spiritual power and moral law. Can be a fatherly figure. The card usually shows the priest wearing a three-tiered crown and holding a triple cross to represent the divine, intellectual and physical worlds.

**Meaning:** Forgiveness and comfort, an advisor – now is the time to learn from other people and stick to established wisdom. Can also represent faith, a teacher or a set of rules. Often, the cards which follow are offering advice.

**Reversed meaning:** Confusion regarding who can be trusted and unhelpful advice. Potentially a crisis of faith, negative conduct. Making your own rules and ignoring established ideas.

## VI The Lovers

This card refers to strong emotions and choices that must be made by the heart. It represents the strength of the human heart and the need to listen to desires. The figures on this card often represent Adam and Eve standing with the Tree of Knowledge.

**Meaning:** Love, reconciliation and physical love. A happy relationship. A decision needs to be made using the heart, choosing true desire over logical thought. A positive change will lead to happier times.

**Reversed meaning:** Indecisiveness or a failure in love. Emotional loss and unwelcome separation from someone or something you care about. It can be a warning that you are making bad choices.

## VII The Chariot

The chariot is often depicted being pulled by a pair of sphinxes, which symbolize the mystery of the future and the forces – both positive and negative – which draw us through life. The two sphinxes may also appear to go in different directions, making the chariot seem harder to control.

**Meaning:** A situation that requires personal strength. Success for the self-reliant. The force of destiny helping you to achieve your goals. Motivation and travel, or unexpected good news.

**Reversed meaning:** Delay and frustration related to goals or travel plans, a lack of focus or sense of being pulled off course.

## VIII Strength

This card shows a woman taming a lion – an act of courage in the face of adversity. The card is ruled by Leo, which indicates honour, reliability, honesty and a sense of purpose.

**Meaning:** Bravery. Physical as well as inner strength. A return to good health if you have been unwell. Others may underestimate the power you have to draw upon.

**Reversed meaning:** Losing your nerve, cowardly behaviour, giving in. A need to overcome your own fears. May signify low self-esteem or being unable to control your emotions.

## IX The Hermit

Often depicted holding a lamp to light the way in the darkness, the Hermit is a card representing loneliness and fear. It is a card of re-evaluation – looking back at past experiences to improve the future.

**Meaning:** It may be time to be alone for a while and reflect on your life. Signifies caution, patience and experience, and warns against sudden changes in course. Represents the idea that you can always learn something new.

**Reversed meaning:** Suggests that you have been alone too long and need to come back out into the world. A warning not to disregard advice from your elders.

## X The Wheel of Fortune

In medieval times, the wheel of fortune was a symbol of human vanity and power. The three creatures around the wheel show the ever-changing status one might have – to be on top one day, and beneath the wheel another.

**Meaning:** An end to problems that you've been going through, and the start of a lucky period. Do not let opportunities pass you by.

**Reversed meaning:** Bad luck and unwelcome surprises. A sign that you are not currently in control of your life, but a reminder that the wheel will eventually turn in your favour again.

## XI Justice

Ruled by Libra and represented by a woman holding a sword in one hand and scales in the other, this card indicates balance and the laws of life. She may be blindfolded to show her impartiality.

**Meaning:** Taking responsibility for your actions. It shows sound judgement and fair outcomes. It signifies that you will succeed in legal affairs if you follow the rules.

**Reversed meaning:** Signifies poor judgement and bad advice. Decisions may not work in your favour. Can represent divorce or other unpleasant legal situations, and can suggest a person who is unwilling to accept responsibility for their mistakes.

## XII The Hanged Man

Though he is hanging upside down, this man does not look frightened or angry. From this position, he can see things as they really are and be at peace. This shows the key theme of this card – reversal. Things will not be the way you expect them to be.

**Meaning:** Life may have to be put on pause for a short time. Rest and reflection is needed, rather than action. You may have to make a sacrifice to gain something new. Events could cause you to feel unbalanced and doubtful.

**Reversed meaning:** Selfishness and impatience, which will hold you back from where you should be. Emotional blackmail. Potentially somebody who only sees things from one perspective.

## XIII Death

Usually depicted as a skeletal figure – sometimes wearing a full suit of armour – on a pale horse. The skeleton shows that the inner self is the strongest part of the physical self.

**Meaning:** This card only signifies death on rare occasions. It is more likely to symbolize change that may seem harsh at the time but is a blessing in disguise. It represents clearing the way for new things.

**Reversed meaning:** May show a change that has been forced, or the loss of a relationship. It could also indicate a refusal to adapt, and serve as a warning against stagnation.

## XIV Temperance

An angelic figure stands in a scene representing all four elements – the card often shows their feet on the earth and wings which allow them to fly in the air and a halo of fire, as they pour water between two jugs. This card is about the balancing of opposing forces.

**Meaning:** Moderation and taking the middle path. Finding balance after a troubled time, or balancing elements which seemed impossible to control before now. It also points to self-control and being adaptable.

**Reversed meaning:** Suggests that something in your life is out of balance and causing stress. This may be a combination of events, people or domestic difficulties.

## XV The Devil

The Devil may be shown with horns, winged or with three eyes. He holds a man and a woman in chains, symbolizing how he rules the physical body.

**Meaning:** Lust, greed and the domination of the physical over the spiritual. Representative of addictive behaviour. May show that you are trapped by repetitive thoughts or unwilling to take responsibility for your actions. An obstacle that cannot yet be overcome. A good card in relation to marriage as it signifies unbreakable bonds.

**Reversed meaning:** Can mean a refusal to change or an inability to see the positive. The overcoming of addictions and regaining positive actions and thoughts.

## XVI The Tower

The depiction of a tower in flames shows that what was considered safe may in fact be dangerous. The sun in the corner suggests that it is always darkest before the dawn and safety may be found again.

**Meaning:** Freedom from old rules and restrictions. A move away from an outdated set of values. Can mean sudden change which is disruptive but nevertheless a blessing – you will come out the other side stronger. The card is a reminder that you cannot control your circumstances, but you can control your reactions.

**Reversed meaning:** Fear of change. Can mean false accusations, or that you will cause a change that is a shock to others.

## XVII The Star

Ruled by Aquarius, this card often shows a woman surrounded by stars, pouring water into a stream and onto the land. It is representative of wishing upon a star.

**Meaning:** A restful card, the Star shows that things are getting better after a challenging time. It suggests insight and the fulfilment of wishes, perhaps in unexpected ways. Also signals good health and a need to trust in the universe.

**Reversed meaning:** Can indicate self-doubt and running away from problems. Pessimism and a lack of opportunity.

## XVIII The Moon

The Moon hovers between two towers. On either side of the moonlit path are a dog and a wolf, the first representing domesticity, and the second representing wildness. A lobster crawls along the path, representing the unconscious mind rising towards the light.

**Meaning:** Use your intuition to deal with a deceptive situation. You are on a challenging path, but you should persist as it will end well. May warn of hidden danger or a struggle to distinguish between real and imagined issues.

**Reversed meaning:** Can warn of bad luck, or imagined problems. Perhaps there are unforeseen dangers and enemies around you.

## XIX The Sun

A smiling sun shines down on sunflowers, often with a child shown riding a white horse. The child is a sign of the innocence associated with this card, and the sunflowers represent the four elements in balance.

**Meaning:** Success, happiness and achievement. A positive outcome for your questions. Can also mean good health, or refer to the summer or sunny places.

**Reversed meaning:** Can suggest an absence of happiness and be a reminder to allow more joy into your life. May also indicate minor setbacks on the path to contentment.

## XX Judgement

A traditionally Christian scene is often depicted, with an angel sounding the last trumpet to call the dead to rise and be judged. This card is primarily symbolic of death and rebirth.

**Meaning:** This is a card of potential. A decision will affect the rest of your life. Forgive yourself for past mistakes and move forward, judging without condemning. Can also signify career success, and that the outcome of your question will happen sooner than expected.

**Reversed meaning:** Fear, ignoring opportunities and being unwavering in your position. A refusal to adapt when change is necessary to progress. Harsh judgement, or the inability to love yourself. A delay in the outcome of your question.

## XXI The World

A naked figure surrounded by a wreath hovers above the Earth. This figure represents someone who is at the end of their spiritual journey and now one with the world. The animals in the corners represent the four elements and the four fixed signs of the zodiac; Aquarius, Taurus, Leo and Scorpio.

**Meaning:** The completion of your task and success in any undertaking. Fulfilment and achievement. The end of one cycle and the start of another. Considered by many as the best card in a Tarot deck, showing that the fight is over and you have won.

**Reversed meaning:** You are yet to achieve your goals. Something is missing in your life. Can signify a feeling of disconnection or a lack of closure.

# THE MINOR ARCANA

## Aces

**Wands meaning:** The beginning of an enterprise – an important new business or relationship. Energy, adventure and confidence.

**Reversed meaning:** Restlessness and a desire for change. Cancelled plans, stagnation and depression. A lack of confidence and a need for others' support.

**Cups meaning:** A fresh start, a budding romance and happy times. Creative success and abundance.

**Reversed meaning:** Emotional instability, bitterness, losing belief in love – perhaps the end of a relationship.

**Swords meaning:** Mental clarity, a time for new ideas and change. Cutting through all obstacles in your path.

**Reversed meaning:** Stress and anxiety, painful truths, fear of new ideas. Misunderstandings and injustice.

**Pentacles meaning:** Achievement. The beginnings of prosperity, and a firm foundation on which to build. Financial luck and monetary gain.

**Reversed meaning:** Greed, jealousy, financial worries and insecurity.

# Twos

**Wands meaning:** Future success. Perhaps a prosperous partnership or new plans that bring positive opportunities.

**Reversed meaning:** Impatience and poor planning. Perhaps signifying problems within a relationship, or lack of fulfilment.

**Cups meaning:** Harmony and balance, especially in matters of the heart. Love and understanding. In a platonic setting, can mean co-operation and friendship.

**Reversed meaning:** Divorce or separation. Misunderstandings, infidelity or disappointment.

**Swords meaning:** Tension. A decision needs to be made but is currently unclear. A difficult alliance, or friendship during a time of adversity.

**Reversed meaning:** Putting off a decision. A lack of responsibility. Can mean betrayal by someone you trust.

**Pentacles meaning:** Resources being spread thin, but still in balance. Adaptability and versatility. May suggest a heavier workload.

**Reversed meaning:** A reckless attitude towards money. Unwise gambling or financial issues. Inability to cope and depression.

# Threes

**Wands meaning:** Luck. Your worries will soon be resolved with a positive outcome. Can signify inspiration and enthusiasm, and in some cases marriage.

**Reversed meaning:** Carelessness and an inability to take charge. Pride and arrogance. Stubborn independence.

---

**Cups meaning:** Family, happiness, celebrations. Sometimes indicates pregnancy and birth, or attendance at a special ceremony (such as a wedding).

**Reversed meaning:** Love triangles. Gossip, overindulgence and false friends. Taking people's feelings for granted. Can suggest unrequited love.

---

**Swords meaning:** A relationship ending badly. Betrayal and ill health – possibly minor surgery is indicated. An obstacle that stood in your way has been removed.

**Reversed meaning:** Confusion, pain and disconnection. Upheaval which causes stress. The start of a long journey of healing.

---

**Pentacles meaning:** Qualifications, talent and expertise that lead to financial gain. Rising above others. Sometimes signifies moving house.

**Reversed meaning:** Self-doubt and wasted talent. Refusal to take risks. Being over-qualified or under-skilled for the situation at hand.

# Fours

**Wands meaning:** Stability, success and moving on to new things. This is the card of the harvest, and shows achievement and wellbeing. Can signify home.

**Reversed meaning:** Family tensions or a period of transition. Unfulfilled hopes and regret.

---

**Cups meaning:** Uncertainty, boredom and frustration. A new start is needed to feel the spark again within a relationship.

**Reversed meaning:** Fear of commitment and unrealistic expectations. Fear of loneliness, depression.

---

**Swords meaning:** Withdrawal or a peaceful interlude. A time to convalesce. Can signify imprisonment or visits to hospitals.

**Reversed meaning:** Burnout due to excessive stress. Illness, confinement. Forced rest.

---

**Pentacles meaning:** Financial security, holding on to your possessions. Financial difficulties will be resolved.

**Reversed meaning:** Either too much spending or too much saving. A grasping attitude, envy.

# Fives

**Wands meaning:** Competition. An exciting challenge, rivalry, a need for flexibility. Maybe a good time for business negotiations.

**Reversed meaning:** Power struggles, petty fighting and selfishness. Misunderstandings and the potential for deception.

---

**Cups meaning:** Disappointment, self-pity and regret. The end of a relationship will allow you to find happiness elsewhere.

**Reversed meaning:** Separation, trust issues and fear of the future. A difficult time will soon come to an end.

---

**Swords meaning:** Failure and loss. Infidelity, unfair battles and unhealthy mental attitudes. Change course or start again to move on.

**Reversed meaning:** Lack of compromise, stubborn pride, discord and destruction. May signify attendance at a funeral.

---

**Pentacles meaning:** Illness, unemployment, the need for guidance. Signifies monetary loss and hardship. You may be looking for support in the wrong place.

**Reversed meaning:** Refusal to accept help, hopelessness. Can indicate bankruptcy or another avoidable loss. A change in attitude is needed.

# Sixes

**Wands meaning:** Victory. Recognition, advancement and success. Ambition fulfilled – your risks will pay off.

**Reversed meaning:** Pride, ego, success for others. Anxiety over delayed success, but prospects are still positive.

**Cups meaning:** Memories, past efforts rewarded, old friends or lovers coming back into your life. May indicate relocation to be closer to your roots.

**Reversed meaning:** Nostalgia, being unable to accept change and move forwards. Outdated feelings or relationships.

**Swords meaning:** Travel, withdrawal, distance, a positive direction to go in. This may be a shared journey.

**Reversed meaning:** Delayed plans, the need for escape, petty problems and the inability to see where you are heading.

**Pentacles meaning:** Generosity, charity, synchronicity. Money put to good use, help received, possibly financial support.

**Reversed meaning:** Selfishness, unwanted gifts, misfortune. Carelessness with money or resources.

## Sevens

**Wands meaning:** Stand your ground. Lots of small problems may occur, but persevere and you will eventually win.

**Reversed meaning:** Being overwhelmed, distractions, giving in. Self-doubt and indecision at a time when self-belief is needed.

---

**Cups meaning:** Hesitation when an important decision must be made. Lack of focus. Need to develop and use intuition.

**Reversed meaning:** Lack of self-belief. Living in a fantasy world or false hope. The loss of opportunity through inaction or poor decision-making.

---

**Swords meaning:** Dishonesty, trickery, suspicions and quarrels. You may need to make a sacrifice to succeed.

**Reversed meaning:** Guilt, jealousy and a lack of trust. Can signify theft.

---

**Pentacles meaning:** Planning, evaluation, effort and hard work. Be patient and persistent.

**Reversed meaning:** Frustration, anxiety and poor planning. Being idle, wasted effort.

# Eights

**Wands meaning:** Life moving faster. Travel, excitement and opportunities. Problems will be quickly resolved. Can mean good news is coming.

**Reversed meaning:** A need to slow down, getting left behind. Premature action, exhaustion and envy.

---

**Cups meaning:** Leaving the past behind. Finding new purpose, changing attitudes and moving on. Following your heart. Can signify travel.

**Reversed meaning:** Separation and anxiety. Outgrowing a relationship. Running away from responsibility or chasing impossible dreams.

---

**Swords meaning:** Restriction. Lack of information. Feeling trapped or hopeless. A run of bad luck. Forget your pride and ask for help.

**Reversed meaning:** A lack of confidence or finding yourself in a cycle of negativity. Taking your frustrations out on others or placing restrictions on yourself.

---

**Pentacles meaning:** Being productive, learning new skills and taking responsibility. Patient effort to reach a long-term goal. Can indicate a new job.

**Reversed meaning:** Laziness, dishonesty, impatience and a refusal to learn. May suggest the loss of employment.

# Nines

**Wands meaning:** Resilience, stability, self-confidence and strength. Be patient and you will succeed.

**Reversed meaning:** Lack of preparation, exhaustion, refusal to compromise and unbending attitudes.

--------------------------------------------------------

**Cups meaning:** Luck, contentment, success. An active social life and good health. Fulfilling relationships and positive communication.

**Reversed meaning:** Laziness, indulgence and excess. Can indicate vanity, or that a partner feels neglected.

--------------------------------------------------------

**Swords meaning:** Nightmares, anxiety, depression and sleepless nights. You may be suffering cruelty or navigating a difficult period to get to something better. Can indicate self-punishment and guilt.

**Reversed meaning:** Reaching your crisis point. Refusing to accept help or see that positive change is possible. Indicates the start of recovery.

--------------------------------------------------------

**Pentacles meaning:** Comfort, financial stability and good sense. You can relax after your hard work. Can also indicate solitude or new purchases.

**Reversed meaning:** Debts, bad investments, theft and loneliness.

# Tens

**Wands meaning:** Heavy burdens. A sense of duty, stress, the refusal to delegate. You will complete your task but the cost may be high.

**Reversed meaning:** Unkindness, lack of responsibility. You may be taken advantage of, or someone may try to disrupt your plans.

---

**Cups meaning:** Contentment. Home, family and harmony that will last. Success and fun – things will work out for the best.

**Reversed meaning:** Betrayal, loss and parenting problems. Losing touch with friends or relatives. Feeling isolated or misunderstood.

---

**Swords meaning:** The end of a negative cycle. Relief, change and hard-earned wisdom. Possibly the need to reach rock-bottom before you can move on.

**Reversed meaning:** Betrayal, melodrama and forced changes. A difficult period that will continue for some time.

---

**Pentacles meaning:** Wealth, investment, confidence, prosperity. A positive family life and can suggest marriage or continuing traditions.

**Reversed meaning:** Financial burdens, family debt, an over-reliance on tradition.

# Pages

**Wands meaning:** A fair-haired young person, an explorer and traveller. They are adaptable, hard-working and can be impulsive. May be a messenger.

**Reversed meaning:** This person is directionless; they want things their way. May be a bringer of bad news.

---

**Cups meaning:** A pale, fair-haired young person. They may be quite androgynous. A dreamer who is trusting, gentle and loving and in need of affection.

**Reversed meaning:** This person is vulnerable, but may also manipulate others.

---

**Swords meaning:** A dark-haired young person who is honest and intelligent, with a sharp wit.

**Reversed meaning:** This person is detached and can be spiteful. May be a liar.

---

**Pentacles meaning:** A dark-haired young person who is enthusiastic, patient and conscientious. They have great prospects. They are often a student. Can signify positive news about money.

**Reversed meaning:** This person is lazy. They are impatient and are often in need of money.

# Knights

**Wands meaning:** A robust, dark young person – usually male. They are an impulsive person, but can be a great friend or partner. Can also indicate moving house.

**Reversed meaning:** This person is hasty and can be jealous. They are argumentative and can be aggressive.

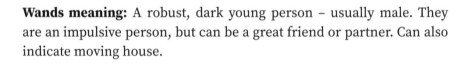

**Cups meaning:** A fair, well-travelled young person – usually male. They are a faithful lover, or a good friend. They are charming and may bring opportunities.

**Reversed meaning:** This person is self-absorbed and may be a heart breaker. Can indicate a lover leaving.

**Swords meaning:** A charming dark-haired young person – usually male. They are always on the move and may leave your life almost as soon as they come into it. They may also be combative.

**Reversed meaning:** This person is closed-minded and secretive. Though they appear to be sincere they are in fact dishonest.

**Pentacles meaning:** A young person with very dark hair – usually male. They are a down-to-earth friend. Someone who doesn't leave things to chance. They accept responsibility and are trustworthy.

**Reversed meaning:** This person is overcautious and doesn't use their imagination.

## Queens

**Wands meaning:** A fair-haired woman who usually has blue or hazel eyes. She is assertive, lively and creative. She may hold a position of responsibility. She loves nature.

**Reversed meaning:** This person is bossy and possessive. She may be jealous.

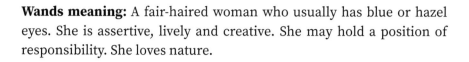

**Cups meaning:** A fair-haired woman, who is accepting and warm. She is devoted to her friends and family. May be creatively gifted and is highly imaginative.

**Reversed meaning:** This person is controlling, demanding and always in need of attention.

**Swords meaning:** A mature woman, possibly a widow, who sees things clearly. She is independent and rational, with a fierce intelligence. Do not underestimate her.

**Reversed meaning:** This person is quick to judge others and can be cruel and jealous.

**Pentacles meaning:** A dark-haired, motherly woman. She is confident, business-minded, kind and charitable. She has a caring personality but may be moody at times.

**Reversed meaning:** This person is superficial. She is suspicious, untrusting and can be possessive.

# Kings

**Wands meaning:** A worldly and mature man, an entrepreneur. Ambitious, strong and honourable. He can be an excellent advisor or a lover.

**Reversed meaning:** This person is intolerant and overbearing. They may be belligerent and are usually a bad advisor.

**Cups meaning:** A mature man who has had great successes. A provider, he is loyal, intelligent and intuitive. He is generous and responsible.

**Reversed meaning:** This person is untrustworthy and secretive. They may be quick to anger, but also easily hurt.

**Swords meaning:** A mature, dark-haired man, an intellectual. He is intelligent and holds authority. Can be challenging. Has a dislike for overt emotions.

**Reversed meaning:** This person is suspicious and unkind. May be dishonest and lead others astray.

**Pentacles meaning:** A dark-haired man who has a great deal of responsibility – potentially a businessman. He is shrewd and even-tempered.

**Reversed meaning:** Impractical and unimaginative, this man makes a bad enemy.

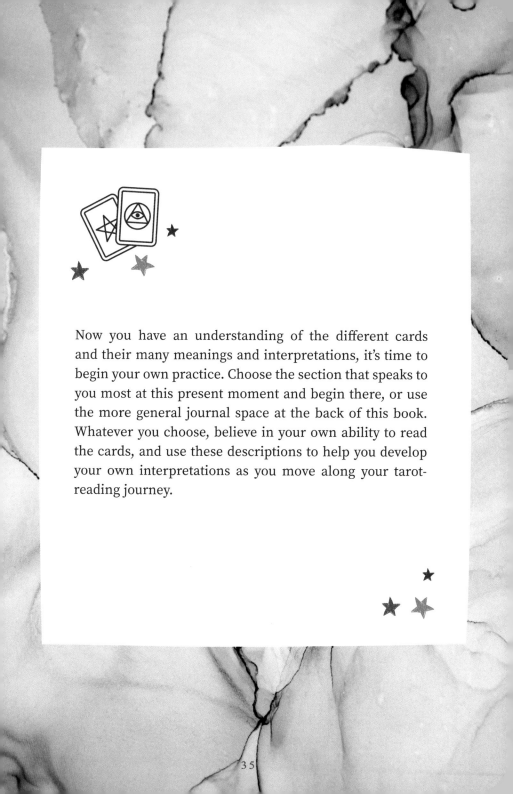

Now you have an understanding of the different cards and their many meanings and interpretations, it's time to begin your own practice. Choose the section that speaks to you most at this present moment and begin there, or use the more general journal space at the back of this book. Whatever you choose, believe in your own ability to read the cards, and use these descriptions to help you develop your own interpretations as you move along your tarot-reading journey.

# TAROT FOR REFLECTION

The first way in which you might use the tarot is to consider events in your life, or for self-reflection. The tarot offer you the chance to ask questions and examine the answers – such as, did you do the right thing, are you on the right path or what can you expect in the near future? For this focus, using a simple three-card spread for past, present and future may give you enough clues to reflect upon. If you'd like to go deeper, you can envisage the year ahead using the calendar spread, which provides one card for each month and a central card that is your main focus, and is excellent for a general reading. Card 1 in this spread is the month you're currently in, so you could repeat the spread monthly and see how your actions and decisions have started to shape potential outcomes.

## Three-card spread

1 The past      2 The present      3 The future/outcome

## Calendar spread

The centre card represents the general feeling or situation, with each of the cards around the circle representing a month. Card 1 will always be the month you are in now, with 2 being the next month and so on until you reach 12.

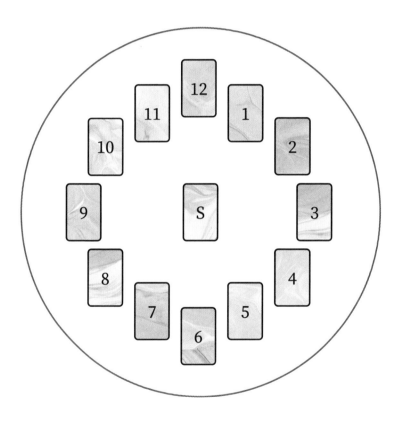

Here are some ideas for questions you might wish to consider, with space to insert your tarot readings or to make notes.

Ask where your current path will lead you.

.............................................................................................

.............................................................................................

.............................................................................................

Look at the year ahead and reflect on how your decisions and actions could affect things.

.............................................................................................

.............................................................................................

.............................................................................................

.............................................................................................

.............................................................................................

Reflect on a recent decision you were unsure about – ask whether you made the right choice.

.............................................................................................

.............................................................................................

.............................................................................................

Reflect on the future you want to manifest and ask the cards if you are on the right path for this.

..................................................................................

..................................................................................

..................................................................................

Think about your inner self – ask the cards if you are being true to yourself.

..................................................................................

..................................................................................

..................................................................................

Use the calendar spread as the horoscope spread, and reflect on your past, present and future as an individual.

..................................................................................

..................................................................................

..................................................................................

..................................................................................

..................................................................................

What question do you have for the cards today?

..................................................................................................

..................................................................................................

Which cards did you draw?

What do you think the cards are trying to tell you?

..............................................................................................

..............................................................................................

..............................................................................................

..............................................................................................

..............................................................................................

..............................................................................................

..............................................................................................

How does this make you feel?

..............................................................................................

..............................................................................................

..............................................................................................

..............................................................................................

..............................................................................................

..............................................................................................

..............................................................................................

What question do you have for the cards today?

......................................................................................................

......................................................................................................

Which cards did you draw?

What do you think the cards are trying to tell you?

......................................................................................

......................................................................................

......................................................................................

......................................................................................

......................................................................................

......................................................................................

......................................................................................

......................................................................................

How does this make you feel?

......................................................................................

......................................................................................

......................................................................................

......................................................................................

......................................................................................

......................................................................................

......................................................................................

......................................................................................

# TAROT FOR DIVINATION

This is the most traditional use for the tarot – asking a question about the future and seeing what the cards envisage. Divination is an art that has many forms – tarot readings are just one of the ways people look to the future, but it is among the most popular for the clear and detailed answers it provides. When asking a question of the cards, it is best to be quite specific rather than general – this will make your answer clearer and give greater focus. For this, a three-card spread is a helpful starting point, but for more detailed answers you could try the cross spread or the horseshoe spread.

## Three-card spread

1 The past      2 The present      3 The future/
                                               outcome

 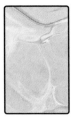 

## Cross spread

1 The past and its influence
2 Obstacles
3 Favourable influences
4 The near future
5 The long term
6 The eventual outcome

## Horseshoe spread

1 The past
2 The present
3 Hidden influences
4 Obstacles
5 Others' attitudes
6 Action to be taken
7 The outcome

Here are some ideas for questions you might wish to consider, with space to insert your tarot readings or to make notes.

Ask whether you are currently on the right path. Decide whether to focus on love, career, family or something else.

..............................................................................................

..............................................................................................

..............................................................................................

Think about a situation that is troubling you. Focus on the problem and the outcome you would like, and use the cards to see if this is the likely result.

..............................................................................................

..............................................................................................

..............................................................................................

..............................................................................................

..............................................................................................

Think about your study or career goals, and ask the cards what it will take to achieve them.

..............................................................................................

..............................................................................................

..............................................................................................

Think about a personal goal or something you want in life. Focus on this and use the cards to see what you need to do to make this achievable.

.....................................................................................

.....................................................................................

.....................................................................................

.....................................................................................

.....................................................................................

.....................................................................................

Think about a relationship you currently have or want to have – this does not need to be a romantic relationship. Use the cards to see whether you will become close with the person in question.

.....................................................................................

.....................................................................................

.....................................................................................

.....................................................................................

.....................................................................................

.....................................................................................

What question do you have for the cards today?

........................................................................................................

........................................................................................................

Which cards did you draw?

What do you think the cards are trying to tell you?

..........................................................................................

..........................................................................................

..........................................................................................

..........................................................................................

..........................................................................................

..........................................................................................

..........................................................................................

..........................................................................................

How does this make you feel?

..........................................................................................

..........................................................................................

..........................................................................................

..........................................................................................

..........................................................................................

..........................................................................................

..........................................................................................

..........................................................................................

What question do you have for the cards today?

........................................................................................................

........................................................................................................

Which cards did you draw?

What do you think the cards are trying to tell you?

..............................................................................

..............................................................................

..............................................................................

..............................................................................

..............................................................................

..............................................................................

..............................................................................

..............................................................................

How does this make you feel?

..............................................................................

..............................................................................

..............................................................................

..............................................................................

..............................................................................

..............................................................................

..............................................................................

..............................................................................

# TAROT FOR SELF-CARE

Self-care isn't just about movie nights and bubble baths – it can also mean taking time to reflect on your life or a question that's troubling you. It is becoming increasingly popular to use the tarot as part of a self-care routine. Reading the cards can give a sense of peace about a difficult situation, or help you focus on what you want to achieve for the future in a relaxing way. Knowing that fate sometimes has a hand in things may also help relieve any tension and stress, helping you realize that sometimes situations are outside of your control. Here, try using the horseshoe spread for a simpler reading, or the fan spread for something more complex.

## Horseshoe spread

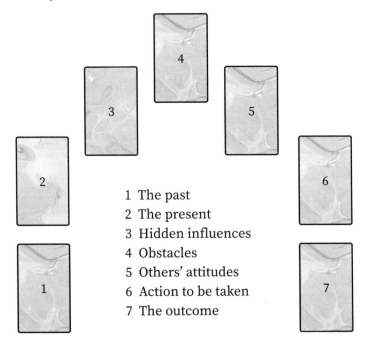

1 The past
2 The present
3 Hidden influences
4 Obstacles
5 Others' attitudes
6 Action to be taken
7 The outcome

# Fan spread

**Centre card:** Select a card to represent the inquirer – a minor arcana court card is usual.

**Group 1:** The inquirer's character, and the recent past

**Group 2:** Love and emotions

**Group 3:** The inquirer's desires

**Group 4:** The inquirer's expectations

**Group 5:** Unknown factors and the unexpected

**Group 6:** The near future

**Group 7:** The long-term future

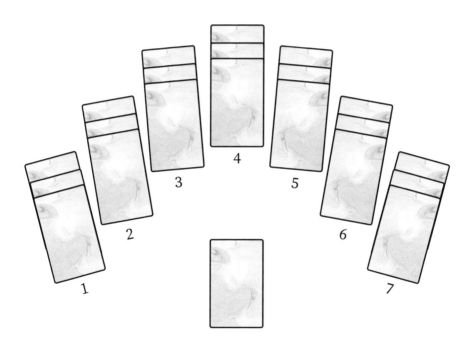

Here are some ideas for questions you might wish to consider, with space to insert your tarot readings or to make notes.

Think about a personal goal or something you want in life. Focus on this and use the cards to see what you need to do to make this achievable.

..........................................................................................................

..........................................................................................................

..........................................................................................................

..........................................................................................................

Focus on your inner peace – even if you don't feel it right now – look for it inside and clear your mind as you deal out the cards for the fan spread.

..........................................................................................................

..........................................................................................................

..........................................................................................................

..........................................................................................................

Ask the cards what you need to do to achieve a sense of happiness.

..........................................................................................................

..........................................................................................................

..........................................................................................................

Think about your inner self – ask the cards if you are being true to yourself.

.........................................................................................................

.........................................................................................................

.........................................................................................................

Think about a situation that is troubling you. Focus on the problem and the outcome you would like, and use the cards to see if this is the likely result.

.........................................................................................................

.........................................................................................................

.........................................................................................................

.........................................................................................................

Focus on a time when you felt stress-free and your heart felt light. Ask the cards whether you are on the path to achieving that sense of calm again, and what you need to do to get there.

.........................................................................................................

.........................................................................................................

.........................................................................................................

What question do you have for the cards today?

......................................................................

......................................................................

Which cards did you draw?

What do you think the cards are trying to tell you?

...........................................................................

...........................................................................

...........................................................................

...........................................................................

...........................................................................

...........................................................................

...........................................................................

How does this make you feel?

...........................................................................

...........................................................................

...........................................................................

...........................................................................

...........................................................................

...........................................................................

...........................................................................

What question do you have for the cards today?

........................................................................................

........................................................................................

Which cards did you draw?

What do you think the cards are trying to tell you?

..................................................................................................

..................................................................................................

..................................................................................................

..................................................................................................

..................................................................................................

..................................................................................................

..................................................................................................

..................................................................................................

How does this make you feel?

..................................................................................................

..................................................................................................

..................................................................................................

..................................................................................................

..................................................................................................

..................................................................................................

..................................................................................................

# TAROT FOR SEEKING ANSWERS

Like divination, one of the more traditional uses for tarot is to ask about how you should proceed with a situation. It is better to ask a specific question than a more general one, especially for smaller card spreads. So, "will I get a promotion at work within the year" is more effective than "am I good at my job", and more likely to result in a clear answer. Many spreads are specially designed to answer questions, and are a great place to start with your tarot readings when looking for answers. Try the basic three-card spread, the horseshoe spread, or the Celtic Cross for more detailed answers.

## Three-card spread

1 The past
2 The present
3 The future/outcome

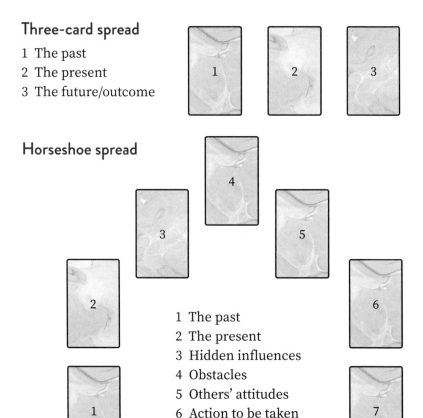

## Horseshoe spread

1 The past
2 The present
3 Hidden influences
4 Obstacles
5 Others' attitudes
6 Action to be taken
7 The outcome

## Celtic Cross spread

1 The heart of the matter
2 The challenge
3 Above you – what is on your mind
4 Below you – the root of the matter
5 Behind you – your immediate past
6 Before you – your immediate future
7 Your attitude to yourself
8 Others' attitudes to you
9 Your hopes and fears
10 The outcome

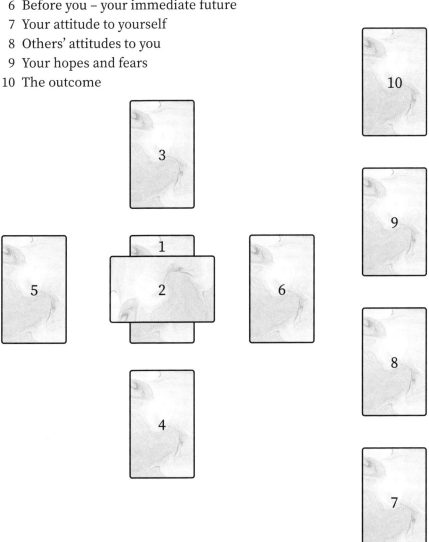

Here are some ideas for questions you might wish to consider, with space to insert your tarot readings or to make notes.

Think about your career. Ask the cards if you will get the promotion or new job you are looking for within the year.

.............................................................................................

.............................................................................................

.............................................................................................

.............................................................................................

Think about your inner self – ask the cards if you are being true to yourself.

.............................................................................................

.............................................................................................

Focus on your partner or a friend. Ask the cards how your relationship will unfold over the next year.

.............................................................................................

.............................................................................................

Concentrate on a new skill you want to learn – ask the cards if you will be successful.

.............................................................................................

.............................................................................................

.............................................................................................

Think about a recent decision you were unsure about – ask whether you made the right choice.

..............................................................................................

..............................................................................................

..............................................................................................

Think about someone you have a difficult relationship with. Ask if, and how, you will be able to improve this relationship.

..............................................................................................

..............................................................................................

..............................................................................................

..............................................................................................

..............................................................................................

Think about your dream goal – the thing you want the most in life. Ask how you will go about achieving it.

..............................................................................................

..............................................................................................

..............................................................................................

..............................................................................................

What question do you have for the cards today?

......................................................................................................

......................................................................................................

Which cards did you draw?

What do you think the cards are trying to tell you?

......................................................................................................

......................................................................................................

......................................................................................................

......................................................................................................

......................................................................................................

......................................................................................................

......................................................................................................

......................................................................................................

How does this make you feel?

......................................................................................................

......................................................................................................

......................................................................................................

......................................................................................................

......................................................................................................

......................................................................................................

......................................................................................................

......................................................................................................

What question do you have for the cards today?

........................................................................................................

........................................................................................................

Which cards did you draw?

What do you think the cards are trying to tell you?

........................................................................................

........................................................................................

........................................................................................

........................................................................................

........................................................................................

........................................................................................

........................................................................................

........................................................................................

How does this make you feel?

........................................................................................

........................................................................................

........................................................................................

........................................................................................

........................................................................................

........................................................................................

........................................................................................

........................................................................................

# TAROT FOR HEALING

Like self-care, tarot is often used for the healing of emotional wounds. Looking back at the past, deep into the present and forwards into the future can help make sense of difficult situations and make them easier to deal with. Knowing that destiny may have had, or still have, a part to play can also reduce feelings of stress or guilt. As tarot can help answer some big questions and provide rare insights into your life, it may help you feel more in tune with who you are and what is happening around you. For this section, try the pentagram spread, which puts you at the centre, or the fan spread for a more complex and detailed reading.

## Pentagram spread

1 You
2 Earth – what grounds you?
3 Air – what inspires you?

4 Fire – what challenges you?
5 Water – what are you learning?
6 Spirit – the outcome

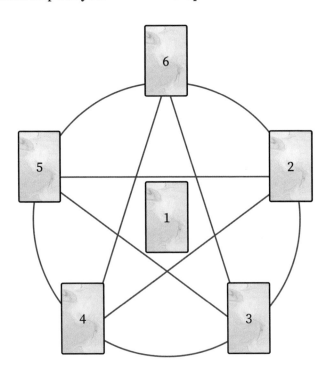

## Fan spread

**Centre card:** Select a card to represent the inquirer – a minor arcana court card is usual.

**Group 1:** The inquirer's character, and the recent past

**Group 2:** Love and emotions

**Group 3:** The inquirer's desires

**Group 4:** The inquirer's expectations

**Group 5:** Unknown factors and the unexpected

**Group 6:** The near future

**Group 7:** The long-term future

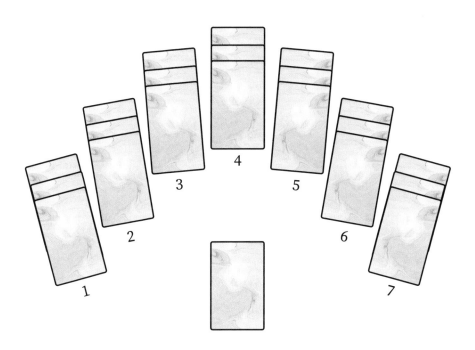

Here are some ideas for questions you might wish to consider, with space to insert your tarot readings or to make notes.

Think about someone you have a difficult relationship with. Ask if and how you will be able to improve this relationship.

.......................................................................................................

.......................................................................................................

.......................................................................................................

.......................................................................................................

.......................................................................................................

.......................................................................................................

Focus on how you are feeling inside. Allow the energy of your personality to flow through you, then use the fan spread to get a deeper insight into yourself.

.......................................................................................................

.......................................................................................................

.......................................................................................................

.......................................................................................................

.......................................................................................................

.......................................................................................................

Think about a recent decision you were unsure about – ask whether you made the right choice.

..................................................................................................

..................................................................................................

Focus on a particularly difficult time in your life. Ask what the likely outcome is, and what you need to do to get past it.

..................................................................................................

..................................................................................................

..................................................................................................

..................................................................................................

Reflect on the future you want to manifest – ask the cards if you are on the right path for this.

..................................................................................................

..................................................................................................

Focus on a time when you felt stress-free and your heart felt light. Ask the cards whether you are on the path to achieving that sense of calm again, and what you need to do to get there.

..................................................................................................

..................................................................................................

What question do you have for the cards today?

.......................................................................................................................

.......................................................................................................................

Which cards did you draw?

What do you think the cards are trying to tell you?

..............................................................................................

..............................................................................................

..............................................................................................

..............................................................................................

..............................................................................................

..............................................................................................

..............................................................................................

..............................................................................................

How does this make you feel?

..............................................................................................

..............................................................................................

..............................................................................................

..............................................................................................

..............................................................................................

..............................................................................................

..............................................................................................

..............................................................................................

What question do you have for the cards today?

...............................................................................

...............................................................................

Which cards did you draw?

What do you think the cards are trying to tell you?

......................................................................................

......................................................................................

......................................................................................

......................................................................................

......................................................................................

......................................................................................

......................................................................................

How does this make you feel?

......................................................................................

......................................................................................

......................................................................................

......................................................................................

......................................................................................

......................................................................................

......................................................................................

# TAROT FOR DECISION-MAKING

When we need to make a decision, we go through a process in our minds which could take seconds, days or weeks. We weigh up pros and cons, and think about the "what ifs" of the situation. Using the tarot when making decisions can help provide clarity and a sense of calm. Given that any choice you make is formed by a series of questions and answers, using spreads that are designed for answering questions can be a big help here. You may also wish to try the calendar spread to get a general idea of how the year ahead will pan out, to help you work out if and when to act on the decision that's currently on your mind.

## Three-card spread

1 The past      2 The present      3 The future/
outcome

## Celtic Cross spread

1 The heart of the matter
2 The challenge
3 Above you – what is on your mind
4 Below you – the root of the matter
5 Behind you – your immediate past
6 Before you – your immediate future
7 Your attitude to yourself
8 Others' attitudes to you
9 Your hopes and fears
10 The outcome

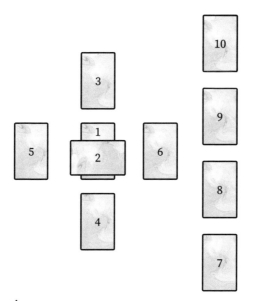

## Calendar spread

The centre card represents the general feeling or situation, with each of the cards around the circle representing a month. Card 1 will always be the month you are in now, with 2 being the next month and so on until you reach 12.

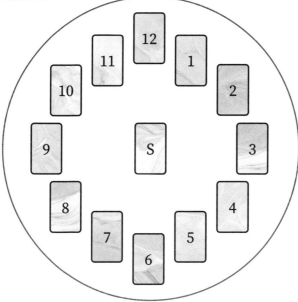

Here are some ideas for questions you might wish to consider, with space to insert your tarot readings or to make notes.

If you're thinking about trying a new hobby but are worried about it taking up too much time or costing too much, ask the cards what the likely outcome will be.

................................................................................................

................................................................................................

................................................................................................

Think about a situation that requires a major decision on your part. Focus on the situation and the outcome you would like – use the cards to see if this is the likely result and how you should decide.

................................................................................................

................................................................................................

................................................................................................

................................................................................................

................................................................................................

If you are thinking about leaving your job or retraining, use the cards to see what the likely outcome will be and help you decide.

................................................................................................

................................................................................................

................................................................................................

Look at the year ahead and reflect on how your decisions and actions could affect things.

..................................................................................................

..................................................................................................

..................................................................................................

..................................................................................................

..................................................................................................

..................................................................................................

If you are thinking about moving house, or relocating, use the cards to help you decide whether this will have the best outcome for you.

..................................................................................................

..................................................................................................

..................................................................................................

Think about a recent decision you were unsure about – ask whether you made the right choice.

..................................................................................................

..................................................................................................

..................................................................................................

What question do you have for the cards today?

.......................................................................................................

.......................................................................................................

Which cards did you draw?

What do you think the cards are trying to tell you?

..........................................................................

..........................................................................

..........................................................................

..........................................................................

..........................................................................

..........................................................................

..........................................................................

How does this make you feel?

..........................................................................

..........................................................................

..........................................................................

..........................................................................

..........................................................................

..........................................................................

..........................................................................

What question do you have for the cards today?

......................................................................................

......................................................................................

Which cards did you draw?

What do you think the cards are trying to tell you?

...................................................................................

...................................................................................

...................................................................................

...................................................................................

...................................................................................

...................................................................................

...................................................................................

How does this make you feel?

...................................................................................

...................................................................................

...................................................................................

...................................................................................

...................................................................................

...................................................................................

...................................................................................

# TAROT FOR SELF-DISCOVERY

We are always on a journey of self-discovery. Every day we have the opportunity to learn more about ourselves and gain profound insights and a deeper relationship with our inner selves. Tarot can help with this process. Using the cards, you can ask questions to help you discover more about your personality, or you can use more general spreads which are designed to reflect who you are now, and who you may become in the future. There are many spreads that may be useful for this, but the Celtic Cross is ideal for questions, and the pyramid or fan spreads can give you a more general reading to help you learn more about your inner self.

## Celtic Cross spread

1  The heart of the matter
2  The challenge
3  Above you – what is on your mind
4  Below you – the root of the matter
5  Behind you – your immediate past
6  Before you – your immediate future
7  Your attitude to yourself
8  Others' attitudes to you
9  Your hopes and fears
10  The outcome

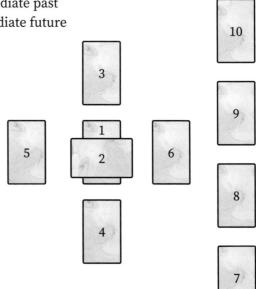

## Pyramid spread

1  Your life as it is now
2  3  The lessons you are learning
4  5  6  Your current beliefs
7  8  9  10  Your foundations (what you are building on)

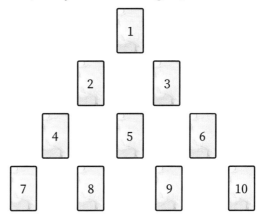

## Fan spread

**Centre card:** Select a card to represent the inquirer – a minor arcana court card is usual.

**Group 1:** The inquirer's character, and the recent past
**Group 2:** Love and emotions
**Group 3:** The inquirer's desires
**Group 4:** The inquirer's expectations
**Group 5:** Unknown factors and the unexpected
**Group 6:** The near future
**Group 7:** The long-term future

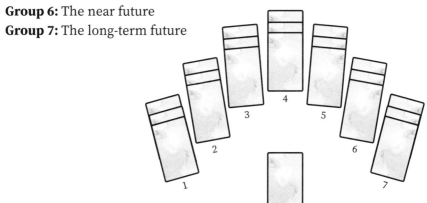

Here are some ideas for questions you might wish to consider, with space to insert your tarot readings or to make notes.

Clear your mind, let the cards take on the essence of you as a person, then use the fan spread to gain insight into your inner self.

.............................................................................................................

.............................................................................................................

.............................................................................................................

.............................................................................................................

.............................................................................................................

.............................................................................................................

Ask the cards what you need to do to achieve a sense of happiness.

.............................................................................................................

.............................................................................................................

.............................................................................................................

Ask whether you are currently on the right path – you can choose whether to focus on love, career, family or something else.

.............................................................................................................

.............................................................................................................

.............................................................................................................

Ask where your current path will lead you.

..........................................................................................

..........................................................................................

..........................................................................................

..........................................................................................

..........................................................................................

Focus on your inner self and ask the cards whether you are currently being true to yourself.

..........................................................................................

..........................................................................................

..........................................................................................

..........................................................................................

Think of a question you have about yourself – this could be about family, relationships, career or just your inner workings. Concentrate on your question and let the cards give you a clear answer.

..........................................................................................

..........................................................................................

..........................................................................................

..........................................................................................

What question do you have for the cards today?

........................................................................................

........................................................................................

Which cards did you draw?

What do you think the cards are trying to tell you?

........................................................................................

........................................................................................

........................................................................................

........................................................................................

........................................................................................

........................................................................................

........................................................................................

How does this make you feel?

........................................................................................

........................................................................................

........................................................................................

........................................................................................

........................................................................................

........................................................................................

........................................................................................

What question do you have for the cards today?

......................................................................................

......................................................................................

Which cards did you draw?

What do you think the cards are trying to tell you?

......................................................................................................

......................................................................................................

......................................................................................................

......................................................................................................

......................................................................................................

......................................................................................................

......................................................................................................

......................................................................................................

How does this make you feel?

......................................................................................................

......................................................................................................

......................................................................................................

......................................................................................................

......................................................................................................

......................................................................................................

......................................................................................................

......................................................................................................

# TAROT FOR ROMANCE

Those who need help with love and romance frequently seek guidance from the tarot. Maybe you want to find out if you and your partner are destined to be together, or if the person you admire feels the same way about you. Perhaps your relationship is going through a rough patch, and you'd like to know when it will improve and what you can do to make it better. Whatever your focus, tarot can lend clarity and reassurance in matters of the heart. For this type of question, try the horseshoe spread or the Celtic Cross.

## Horseshoe spread

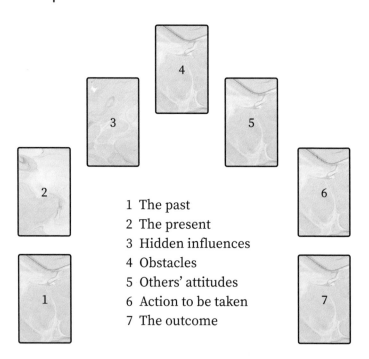

1 The past
2 The present
3 Hidden influences
4 Obstacles
5 Others' attitudes
6 Action to be taken
7 The outcome

## Celtic Cross spread

1 The heart of the matter
2 The challenge
3 Above you – what is on your mind
4 Below you – the root of the matter
5 Behind you – your immediate past
6 Before you – your immediate future
7 Your attitude to yourself
8 Others' attitudes to you
9 Your hopes and fears
10 The outcome

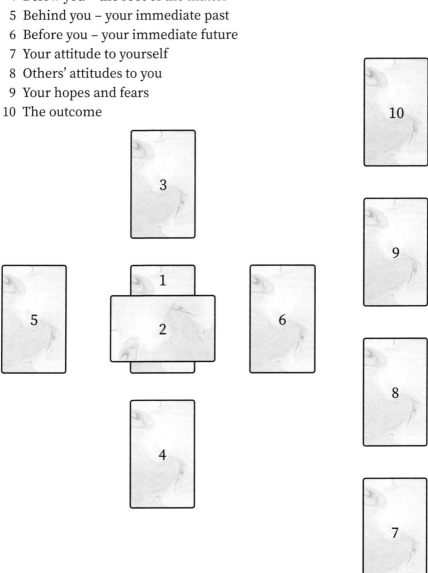

Here are some ideas for questions you might wish to consider, with space to insert your tarot readings or to make notes.

If you are wondering if you and your partner are destined to stay together, ask the cards what the future holds for you.

......................................................................................................

......................................................................................................

......................................................................................................

If you are having difficulty in your relationship, ask the cards for clarity on how to move forwards.

......................................................................................................

......................................................................................................

......................................................................................................

......................................................................................................

......................................................................................................

Think about the person your heart is set on – ask the cards if they feel the same way about you.

......................................................................................................

......................................................................................................

......................................................................................................

If you are considering a potential proposal, focus on marriage and ask the cards if this is in your near future.

......................................................................................

......................................................................................

......................................................................................

If you're planning to make a particular romantic gesture, ask the cards if it will be a success.

......................................................................................

......................................................................................

......................................................................................

If you've been single for some time and wonder if love is around the corner, keep love at the centre of your thoughts and ask the cards what the future will bring.

......................................................................................

......................................................................................

......................................................................................

......................................................................................

......................................................................................

What question do you have for the cards today?

........................................................................

........................................................................

Which cards did you draw?

What do you think the cards are trying to tell you?

.......................................................................................................

.......................................................................................................

.......................................................................................................

.......................................................................................................

.......................................................................................................

.......................................................................................................

.......................................................................................................

.......................................................................................................

How does this make you feel?

.......................................................................................................

.......................................................................................................

.......................................................................................................

.......................................................................................................

.......................................................................................................

.......................................................................................................

.......................................................................................................

What question do you have for the cards today?

........................................................................................................

........................................................................................................

Which cards did you draw?

What do you think the cards are trying to tell you?

..................................................................................................

..................................................................................................

..................................................................................................

..................................................................................................

..................................................................................................

..................................................................................................

..................................................................................................

..................................................................................................

How does this make you feel?

..................................................................................................

..................................................................................................

..................................................................................................

..................................................................................................

..................................................................................................

..................................................................................................

..................................................................................................

..................................................................................................

# TAROT FOR FRIENDSHIP

Like romantic relationships, our friendships are at the heart of who we are and how we spend our time. This can be a source of both positive and negative energy. Like any relationship, friendships can sometimes have difficult patches and, inevitably, there are occasions where two people simply grow apart. Tarot can offer insight into our friendships, and comfort when there is tension between friends. If you're wondering if a friendship is becoming something more, tarot can help you focus your energies and find answers about how to move forwards. For this section, the cross spread or the horseshoe spread would be ideal alongside specific questions.

## Cross spread

1 The past and its influence
2 Obstacles
3 Favourable influences
4 The near future
5 The long term
6 The eventual outcome

# Horseshoe spread

1 The past
2 The present
3 Hidden influences
4 Obstacles
5 Others' attitudes
6 Action to be taken
7 The outcome

Here are some ideas for questions you might wish to consider, with space to insert your tarot readings or to make notes.

Think about someone you have a difficult relationship with. Ask if and how you will be able to improve this relationship.

..............................................................................................

..............................................................................................

..............................................................................................

..............................................................................................

Focus on a friend – ask the cards how your relationship will unfold over the next year.

..............................................................................................

..............................................................................................

..............................................................................................

Think about a friendship you currently have or want to have. Use the cards to see whether you will become closer with the person in question.

..............................................................................................

..............................................................................................

..............................................................................................

..............................................................................................

If you hope that a friendship will develop into something more, keep the friend in mind and ask the cards how your relationship will grow.

....................................................................................

....................................................................................

....................................................................................

If you have a friend who is going through a difficult period in their life, ask the cards what you can do to help them.

....................................................................................

....................................................................................

....................................................................................

If there is someone in your friendship group who is causing difficulties, ask the cards what you can do to help them integrate with the group, or if you need to move away from this friendship.

....................................................................................

....................................................................................

....................................................................................

....................................................................................

....................................................................................

What question do you have for the cards today?

........................................................................................

........................................................................................

Which cards did you draw?

What do you think the cards are trying to tell you?

..............................................................................

..............................................................................

..............................................................................

..............................................................................

..............................................................................

..............................................................................

..............................................................................

..............................................................................

How does this make you feel?

..............................................................................

..............................................................................

..............................................................................

..............................................................................

..............................................................................

..............................................................................

..............................................................................

..............................................................................

What question do you have for the cards today?

......................................................................

......................................................................

Which cards did you draw?

What do you think the cards are trying to tell you?

..............................................................................................

..............................................................................................

..............................................................................................

..............................................................................................

..............................................................................................

..............................................................................................

..............................................................................................

..............................................................................................

How does this make you feel?

..............................................................................................

..............................................................................................

..............................................................................................

..............................................................................................

..............................................................................................

..............................................................................................

..............................................................................................

..............................................................................................

# TAROT FOR CAREER

Our working life can consume a lot of our time and energy, and play a big part in how we define ourselves. Insight and guidance into our careers can often be helpful. This can be about whether you are choosing the right job, if you should retrain, whether you'll get a promotion, or a whole host of other questions. Whatever you feel the need to ask about, tarot readings can help you feel more secure in your choices and give you peace of mind. They can also help with a difficult decision, helping you to finally decide on one course of action. For career questions, the Celtic Cross would be a great starting place, with the horseshoe also working well.

## Celtic Cross spread

1  The heart of the matter
2  The challenge
3  Above you – what is on your mind
4  Below you – the root of the matter
5  Behind you – your immediate past
6  Before you – your immediate future
7  Your attitude to yourself
8  Others' attitudes to you
9  Your hopes and fears
10  The outcome

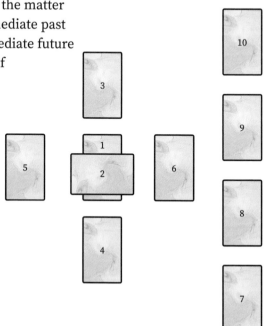

## Horseshoe spread

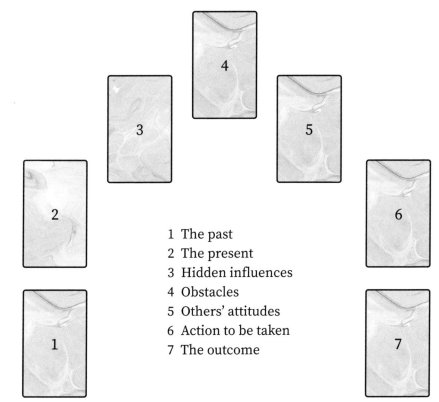

1 The past
2 The present
3 Hidden influences
4 Obstacles
5 Others' attitudes
6 Action to be taken
7 The outcome

Here are some ideas for questions you might wish to consider, with space to insert your tarot readings or to make notes.

If you are thinking about leaving your job or retraining, use the cards to see what the likely outcome will be.

..........................................................................................

..........................................................................................

..........................................................................................

Think about your dream job – the thing you want to do the most in life. Ask how you will go about achieving it.

..........................................................................................

..........................................................................................

..........................................................................................

..........................................................................................

..........................................................................................

Think about your current job – ask the cards whether you are in the right place for you.

..........................................................................................

..........................................................................................

..........................................................................................

Focus on a new skill you want to learn – ask the cards if you will be successful.

........................................................................................

........................................................................................

Think about your career goals and ask the cards what it will take to achieve them.

........................................................................................

........................................................................................

........................................................................................

If you're aiming for a promotion, ask the cards if this is in your near future.

........................................................................................

........................................................................................

........................................................................................

If you're having difficulties with your employer or a colleague, ask the cards how to move forwards and create a better relationship.

........................................................................................

........................................................................................

........................................................................................

What question do you have for the cards today?

..........................................................................................

..........................................................................................

Which cards did you draw?

What do you think the cards are trying to tell you?

..............................................................................................

..............................................................................................

..............................................................................................

..............................................................................................

..............................................................................................

..............................................................................................

..............................................................................................

..............................................................................................

How does this make you feel?

..............................................................................................

..............................................................................................

..............................................................................................

..............................................................................................

..............................................................................................

..............................................................................................

..............................................................................................

..............................................................................................

What question do you have for the cards today?

........................................................................................

........................................................................................

Which cards did you draw?

What do you think the cards are trying to tell you?

...............................................................................................

...............................................................................................

...............................................................................................

...............................................................................................

...............................................................................................

...............................................................................................

...............................................................................................

How does this make you feel?

...............................................................................................

...............................................................................................

...............................................................................................

...............................................................................................

...............................................................................................

...............................................................................................

...............................................................................................

...............................................................................................

# NOTES

# MY
# TAROT
# READINGS

What question do you have for the cards today?

...................................................................................

...................................................................................

Which cards did you draw?

What do you think the cards are trying to tell you?

..........................................................................................

..........................................................................................

..........................................................................................

..........................................................................................

..........................................................................................

..........................................................................................

..........................................................................................

..........................................................................................

How does this make you feel?

..........................................................................................

..........................................................................................

..........................................................................................

..........................................................................................

..........................................................................................

..........................................................................................

..........................................................................................

..........................................................................................

What question do you have for the cards today?

........................................................................................................

........................................................................................................

Which cards did you draw?

What do you think the cards are trying to tell you?

..............................................................................

..............................................................................

..............................................................................

..............................................................................

..............................................................................

..............................................................................

..............................................................................

How does this make you feel?

..............................................................................

..............................................................................

..............................................................................

..............................................................................

..............................................................................

..............................................................................

..............................................................................

What question do you have for the cards today?

..............................................................................

..............................................................................

Which cards did you draw?

What do you think the cards are trying to tell you?

....................................................................................................

....................................................................................................

....................................................................................................

....................................................................................................

....................................................................................................

....................................................................................................

....................................................................................................

How does this make you feel?

....................................................................................................

....................................................................................................

....................................................................................................

....................................................................................................

....................................................................................................

....................................................................................................

....................................................................................................

What question do you have for the cards today?

·······························································································

·······························································································

Which cards did you draw?

What do you think the cards are trying to tell you?

..........................................................................................

..........................................................................................

..........................................................................................

..........................................................................................

..........................................................................................

..........................................................................................

..........................................................................................

..........................................................................................

How does this make you feel?

..........................................................................................

..........................................................................................

..........................................................................................

..........................................................................................

..........................................................................................

..........................................................................................

..........................................................................................

..........................................................................................

What question do you have for the cards today?

........................................................................................................

........................................................................................................

Which cards did you draw?

What do you think the cards are trying to tell you?

..................................................................................................

..................................................................................................

..................................................................................................

..................................................................................................

..................................................................................................

..................................................................................................

..................................................................................................

How does this make you feel?

..................................................................................................

..................................................................................................

..................................................................................................

..................................................................................................

..................................................................................................

..................................................................................................

..................................................................................................

..................................................................................................

What question do you have for the cards today?

......................................................................................................

......................................................................................................

Which cards did you draw?

What do you think the cards are trying to tell you?

...................................................................................................

...................................................................................................

...................................................................................................

...................................................................................................

...................................................................................................

...................................................................................................

...................................................................................................

How does this make you feel?

...................................................................................................

...................................................................................................

...................................................................................................

...................................................................................................

...................................................................................................

...................................................................................................

...................................................................................................

What question do you have for the cards today?

........................................................................................................................

........................................................................................................................

Which cards did you draw?

What do you think the cards are trying to tell you?

..............................................................................

..............................................................................

..............................................................................

..............................................................................

..............................................................................

..............................................................................

..............................................................................

..............................................................................

How does this make you feel?

..............................................................................

..............................................................................

..............................................................................

..............................................................................

..............................................................................

..............................................................................

..............................................................................

..............................................................................

What question do you have for the cards today?

........................................................................................................

........................................................................................................

Which cards did you draw?

What do you think the cards are trying to tell you?

......................................................................................

......................................................................................

......................................................................................

......................................................................................

......................................................................................

......................................................................................

......................................................................................

......................................................................................

How does this make you feel?

......................................................................................

......................................................................................

......................................................................................

......................................................................................

......................................................................................

......................................................................................

......................................................................................

......................................................................................

What question do you have for the cards today?

....................................................................................

....................................................................................

Which cards did you draw?

What do you think the cards are trying to tell you?

..............................................................................

..............................................................................

..............................................................................

..............................................................................

..............................................................................

..............................................................................

..............................................................................

..............................................................................

How does this make you feel?

..............................................................................

..............................................................................

..............................................................................

..............................................................................

..............................................................................

..............................................................................

..............................................................................

..............................................................................

What question do you have for the cards today?

........................................................................................................

........................................................................................................

Which cards did you draw?

What do you think the cards are trying to tell you?

..................................................................................................

..................................................................................................

..................................................................................................

..................................................................................................

..................................................................................................

..................................................................................................

..................................................................................................

..................................................................................................

How does this make you feel?

..................................................................................................

..................................................................................................

..................................................................................................

..................................................................................................

..................................................................................................

..................................................................................................

..................................................................................................

..................................................................................................

What question do you have for the cards today?

...........................................................................................................

...........................................................................................................

Which cards did you draw?

What do you think the cards are trying to tell you?

.......................................................................................

.......................................................................................

.......................................................................................

.......................................................................................

.......................................................................................

.......................................................................................

.......................................................................................

How does this make you feel?

.......................................................................................

.......................................................................................

.......................................................................................

.......................................................................................

.......................................................................................

.......................................................................................

.......................................................................................

What question do you have for the cards today?

......................................................................................................

......................................................................................................

Which cards did you draw?

What do you think the cards are trying to tell you?

..........................................................................................
..........................................................................................
..........................................................................................
..........................................................................................
..........................................................................................
..........................................................................................
..........................................................................................
..........................................................................................

How does this make you feel?

..........................................................................................
..........................................................................................
..........................................................................................
..........................................................................................
..........................................................................................
..........................................................................................
..........................................................................................

What question do you have for the cards today?

........................................................................

........................................................................

Which cards did you draw?

What do you think the cards are trying to tell you?

...........................................................................................

...........................................................................................

...........................................................................................

...........................................................................................

...........................................................................................

...........................................................................................

...........................................................................................

How does this make you feel?

...........................................................................................

...........................................................................................

...........................................................................................

...........................................................................................

...........................................................................................

...........................................................................................

...........................................................................................

What question do you have for the cards today?

........................................................................................

........................................................................................

Which cards did you draw?

What do you think the cards are trying to tell you?

..................................................................................

..................................................................................

..................................................................................

..................................................................................

..................................................................................

..................................................................................

..................................................................................

How does this make you feel?

..................................................................................

..................................................................................

..................................................................................

..................................................................................

..................................................................................

..................................................................................

..................................................................................

What question do you have for the cards today?

......................................................................................................

......................................................................................................

Which cards did you draw?

What do you think the cards are trying to tell you?

..................................................................................

..................................................................................

..................................................................................

..................................................................................

..................................................................................

..................................................................................

..................................................................................

How does this make you feel?

..................................................................................

..................................................................................

..................................................................................

..................................................................................

..................................................................................

..................................................................................

..................................................................................

What question do you have for the cards today?

..................................................................................................

..................................................................................................

Which cards did you draw?

What do you think the cards are trying to tell you?

..................................................................................................

..................................................................................................

..................................................................................................

..................................................................................................

..................................................................................................

..................................................................................................

..................................................................................................

..................................................................................................

How does this make you feel?

..................................................................................................

..................................................................................................

..................................................................................................

..................................................................................................

..................................................................................................

..................................................................................................

..................................................................................................

..................................................................................................

What question do you have for the cards today?

.............................................................................................

.............................................................................................

Which cards did you draw?

What do you think the cards are trying to tell you?

........................................................................................

........................................................................................

........................................................................................

........................................................................................

........................................................................................

........................................................................................

........................................................................................

How does this make you feel?

........................................................................................

........................................................................................

........................................................................................

........................................................................................

........................................................................................

........................................................................................

........................................................................................

........................................................................................

What question do you have for the cards today?

......................................................................................

......................................................................................

Which cards did you draw?

What do you think the cards are trying to tell you?

..................................................................................................
..................................................................................................
..................................................................................................
..................................................................................................
..................................................................................................
..................................................................................................
..................................................................................................
..................................................................................................

How does this make you feel?

..................................................................................................
..................................................................................................
..................................................................................................
..................................................................................................
..................................................................................................
..................................................................................................
..................................................................................................

What question do you have for the cards today?

.........................................................................................................

.........................................................................................................

Which cards did you draw?

What do you think the cards are trying to tell you?

..............................................................................................................

..............................................................................................................

..............................................................................................................

..............................................................................................................

..............................................................................................................

..............................................................................................................

..............................................................................................................

..............................................................................................................

How does this make you feel?

..............................................................................................................

..............................................................................................................

..............................................................................................................

..............................................................................................................

..............................................................................................................

..............................................................................................................

..............................................................................................................

..............................................................................................................

What question do you have for the cards today?

......................................................................................................

......................................................................................................

Which cards did you draw?

What do you think the cards are trying to tell you?

.....................................................................................

.....................................................................................

.....................................................................................

.....................................................................................

.....................................................................................

.....................................................................................

.....................................................................................

How does this make you feel?

.....................................................................................

.....................................................................................

.....................................................................................

.....................................................................................

.....................................................................................

.....................................................................................

.....................................................................................

# FINAL WORD

We hope you have enjoyed learning about the tarot and putting your knowledge to use in your own readings. The process of filling in this journal was a commitment that hopefully rewarded you with valuable insights and clarity. Tarot reading is a skill like any other, so keep practising, and before long you'll be able to read the cards without looking back at prompts. If you wish to continue, why not get a blank journal and use it to draw your spreads and outcomes? In time, you might like to try reading somebody else's cards and see how your revelations can help to unravel questions and provide solutions. You might also like to research new spreads and experiment to find what suits you best. Whatever you do next, we wish you all the best as you embark on this magical and lifelong journey into the wisdom of tarot.

# THE LITTLE BOOK OF TAROT

Xanna Eve Chown

978-1-78685-798-9

## HAVE YOU EVER WONDERED WHAT FATE HAS IN STORE FOR YOU?

For hundreds of years, tarot cards have been used as a tool for divination, and a way to shed light on life's questions and challenges. With an introduction to the 78 cards and their symbols, advice on choosing your deck and tips on how to prepare and read your cards, *The Little Book of Tarot* has everything you'll need to gain your first glimpse into the misty realms of the future... what message will the cards hold for you?

Have you enjoyed this book?
If so, find us on Facebook at **Summersdale Publishers**,
on Twitter at **@Summersdale** and on Instagram at
**@summersdalebooks** and get in touch.
We'd love to hear from you!

# www.summersdale.com

## IMAGE CREDITS